All
Stories
Are True ...
Some Actually Happened

Soul Snorkeling: Stories and Art
for looking below the surface

*For Ray who has always supported my wild ideas,
and Stephanie who has always told me to tell my own stories.*

Visit www.booksurge.com to order additional copies.
To arrange *Soul Snorkeling* programs:
www: soulsnorkeling.net or
email: soulsnorkeling@gmail.com

All
Stories
Are True ...
Some Actually Happened

Soul Snorkeling: Stories and Art
for looking below the surface

Sheila S. Otto

A sense of wonder helps make a sewer cover into a canvas if we have eyes to see.

> Am I open to being surprised?
> Do I look for the positive, the beautiful?
> Where does the negative block my sense of wonder and awe?

Contents

Introduction   1
Problems and Solutions   3
Stuffed   4
Frog Town   5
Growth Enhancement   7
The Telephone   8
Nasruddin   9
Fish Story   11
Tears   12
And the Envelope Says …   13
Blind?   15
Channel Surfing   16
Efficiency   17
Upon This Rock   19
Distraction   20
Hammer Head   21
Star Bucks Techies   23
Markings   24
Perspective   25
Antiques Roadshow   27
Medical Musings   28
What is the Sound of … ?   29
Which Car Are You Driving?   31
Song and Dance   32

Coke	33
Sudoku	35
Economics 101	36
Howz That Spelled?	37
African Clinic	39
Training Methods	40
How May I Help You?	41
Book of Common Prayer	43
Smell the Flowers	44
Plane Talk	45
Salt of the Hearth	47
Namaste	48
Your Space	50
Photos and Art	53
Warning Label	54

Introduction

Storytellers believe that the shortest line between the head and the heart is a story. They also agree that all stories are true, some actually happened.

As a storyteller, I love to tell and write stories of different spiritual traditions. As a spiritual director for two decades, I encourage people to look deeply into their own stories. Both paths have led me to create this collection of stories and art as a way for you to gaze at the images and read the stories contemplatively. I hope they will take you on your own inner journey.

All traditions of spirituality praise the qualities of the seeker whose eyes and ears are open, who sees the holy in the ordinary, and who takes the time to be in silent awe before the wonders that are everywhere.

My photographs, paintings and drawings, and stories are an invitation to go below the surface, to look for the beauty and wisdom that you already know within your experience and soul. I love snorkeling in tropical waters where there is unending mystery and magic, so I like to refer to this pondering as *soul snorkeling.*

Breathe deeply, dive in!

Sheila Otto

Whether the glass is full, half full or half empty, can I be grateful?

Problems and Solutions

The young mother had recently given a rudimentary explanation of sanitary products to her three-year-old daughter. The little one came running into the house from her daddy's workshop.

"Mommy, Mommy! Quick, Daddy's bleeding. He needs a tampon."

Because you see the problem, doesn't mean the solution you know is the best solution.

Stuffed

The collection of stuffed animals filled the little girl's room to rival the crowded conditions Noah created on the ark, but without his waste disposal problems.

Whenever her rich uncle visited her vast collection, he used to say, "You can never have too much money or too many toys."

Her aunt, recently returned from the Peace Corps, believed the collection did have a waste problem.

When is enough enough?

> St. John of the Cross, 15th century Spanish mystic and poet wrote:
>> To reach satisfaction in all,
>> desire its possession in nothing.
>> To come to possess all,
>> desire the possession of nothing.

Frog Town

The international frog conference met by a murky pond near Toledo* filled with frogs of all varieties. Gathered there were tree frogs, pond frogs, well-frogs, green and brown and multi-colored frogs.

The keynoter was a distinguished scholar from the Script's Academy of Oceanography. His elaborate PowerPoint presentation on the miracles of ocean life drew no applause.

The miracles he described were completely outside the world view and experience of all the attendees.

We can't conceive of miracles if we don't believe there is a mystery bigger than ourselves.

* *Toledo, Ohio, is known affectionately as Frogtown because much of the original settlement was swampy. This story was inspired by Anthony de Mello's story in <u>One Minute Wisdom</u> that a well-frog can't understand the ocean.*

The water lily is a natural at reflection.
How can I be more mindful in my daily life?
How do I name and accept my shadow, my
undeveloped and denied self?

Growth Enhancement

The small group of friends who had gathered for lunch after Grandpa's funeral were a confused. A family member dipped a spoon into a bowl containing a gray substance and asked if they would like a bit of Grandpa to take home in one of the tiny white boxes she was filling.

The friends had come to expect surprises, still they found this offer out of the ordinary. To explain this unusual gesture, the daughter explained further.

"Grandpa spread Grandmama's ashes over his rose garden last spring and his roses bloomed more beautifully than ever. We wanted to let Grandpa help *your* gardens grow this year."

What legacy do we want to leave behind? Is it about how we have encouraged growth in others? Is it that we have made a difference?

The Telephone

At the monthly gathering of the *Ladies Night Out,* the gals were mixing Margaritas, Martinis, and Marriage.

"You can't believe my husband. He says you should never … ." A chorus of "My husband says the only way …" cropped up all around the table.

The blonde at the end of the table said, "It was like that when I was growing up. We had five kids and my father hated for us to be on the phone more than three minutes. He'd insist, 'State your business and get off.'

Mom would try to explain her tolerance of our lengthy phone calls. 'Your Dad grew up with only one phone in his village. It was at the Post Office and people only used it to call the doctor.'

My mother had grown up using the phone without limits because her mother's father owned the regional telephone company in Kansas in the 20s and 30s and that family always took the telephone for granted."

Our family of origin gives us beliefs we think are absolutes. We enter marriage believing them, only to find out our spouse has different "true" beliefs. The trick in marriage is to create our own jointly shared beliefs which our children will have to unlearn in their marriages.

Nasruddin *

When a therapist told Nasruddin that pornography
was ruining many marriages, he planned to stir public
awareness of the dangers. He decided to make a very
obvious scene of thumbing through a pornographic
magazine by the town fountain where he'd be seen.

When people acted scandalized, he merely explained,
"Oh, it's so much quicker, less messy, and quite satisfying."

He issued a dinner invitation to his scoffing critics.
When they arrived, he served each guest an appetizer:
the current issue of *Gourmet Magazine*. Next came the
entrée: *Bon Appétit* accompanied by a vintage issue of
Wine Spectator. Dessert was a crumbled, torn copy of
Healthy Eating.

The gentlemen went home hungry, deleted their porn
web sites, and discovered the deep joy of making love
to their wives.

Later that evening Nasruddin and his wife delighted in
the banquet of each other as they laughed and nibbled
sweets from the enamelled tray by their bed.

**Any addiction deadens the senses to the power of
a natural high.**

** Nasruddin is a folk hero in much of the Middle East. He is based on
a mysterious character of the the 13th century (1209?-1285?) born in
Turkey. His stories are either foolishness or wisdom tales, depending on
the listener's point of view.*

Sometimes there is a temptation to escape painful times. How can I navigate the rough waters if I don't stay focused on the moment?

Is there something that has "beached" my dreams?

How can I reset my course?

A Fish Story

NOAA, the National Oceanic and Atmospheric Administration, is a federal agency focused on the condition of the oceans and the atmosphere. "Can fish distinguish color?" is a a frequently asked question on their website. Their official answer is, "Most fish are colorblind, despite the opinions of many sportfishermen."

The sportfishing marketing teams know their customers well. There isn't a fisherman alive who doesn't already have a rainbow of lures in the tackle box. But if today the other guys on the boat are catching them on red or blue or green lures, the first thing he'll do is go buy some new ones of that color.

Scientific evidence doesn't stand a chance against ingrained beliefs.

Tears

A mother who had lost a son and a brother during the same week in a terrorist attack sought consolation from the village healer.

The healer put her arm around the grieving woman and told her, "I cannot take away your anger or your pain or dry your tears. I can only teach you how those tears can water the holy ground on which you walk in the hope that love will one day sprout anew."

And the Envelope Says ...

Susie was given up for adoption at 18 months. Seven decades later she decided to search for her birth mother. The Nevada agency she contacted said it was an easy match. Their records, dating back to the 70s, showed that her mother had attempted without success to find her.

When she met her 75-year-old half-brother for the first time, he showed Sue an empty envelope from the agency that their mother had never thrown out. It was evidence of her mother's attempt to reconnect. Because her son never knew his mother's full story, never knew about an older sibling, he hadn't known why that envelope was so important until that moment.

Finding a family she never knew gave Sue new identity. It was the empty envelope, evidence of love's search, of a mother's aching heart, that gave her lasting peace. "My mother wanted to find me; she always loved me." That proof fills her heart.

When we finally recognize how God, our mother and father, has always loved us, even when we have thought ourselves abandoned, we know our true identity as God's beloved.

- 13 -

The temple bell, the church bell, the alarm clock
all call us to wake up and know what time it is.
When we do that it is the beginning of awareness.
What time is it? Now, not tomorrow.
Where am I? Here, not in the last week's
difficult meeting.

Blind?

The saffron-robed abbot loved to use the drive-up ATM machine. He was always amused to watch the money spill out like magic. He would sometimes drive up to the machine and use the Braille panel. When the confused teller queried him, he would say, with a twinkle in his eye, that he knew he was blind to many of his shortcomings and needed to be reminded regularly of that blindness.

He would comment to his bemused passenger that he had often wanted to buy one of those huge convex mirror sometimes found on roadways with a "Blind Corner" warning sign. He wanted to put one by the entrance to the prayer hall, but he questioned if monastery visitors would, even then, notice their own blind corners.

What annoys us in others is often a mirror of our own shortcomings. It is easy to be blind to such evidence.

Channel Surfing

While visiting the U.S. for the first time, the guru was fascinated by the television remote and how it was used.

It was for him the perfect model of detachment. He saw it in use and realized that you never had to become engaged in the passing image. He thought it was the perfect image to use for explaining meditation.

His students were a bit embarrassed at his use of the image. They didn't think he understood the technology well enough to use it as a metaphor.

He just laughed and said, "Let all distracting images run by the screen of your mind, don't stop to pay attention, and you will discover the secret of peace and meditation."

We get hooked on stories that aren't our own. We get stuck in our old stories. We create stories to worry about. How can we gain control of the stories we tell ourselves?

Efficiency

The 20th century Trappist monk and mystic, Thomas Merton, once said that the greatest threat to spirituality was not moral decay or declining church influence, but efficiency.

"How come? I pride myself on cramming my day full of projects. I am terrific at multi-tasking. I can make a phone call while driving, doing my expense account, ironing, e-mailing or searching my files and listening to a CD. I am efficient and it is good. It is *essential* in my busy life."

It's not that we are bad people, just busy people. Jesus told a story of the banquet which people were too busy to attend. Without making time to wonder, to be grateful and appreciative, we, too, are likely to miss the feast.

The way something appears to me may not be
what you see because we see it from a different
angle, in a different light.

How can I begin to appreciate other
viewpoints?

Can I accept "both/and" instead of
only "either/or?"

Upon This Rock

Sister Sujita, the Indian woman who leads the international order of Catholic women religious, the Sisters of Notre Dame, tells this story on herself.

While working with poor village women in India she invited a villager to join her in prayer at mass. Later the woman reciprocated and invited Sister to a local religious ceremony.

The ceremony seemed focused on a pile of stones around which rituals were performed. After the ceremony Sister asked, "How is it that you seem to worship stones?"

The woman, with a hint of a smile, asked, "How is it that you seem to worship bread?"

We tend to see as holy, only those things our own culture names as holy.

Distraction

The rabbi loved to teach with stories. He told his congregation a story from his own life experience and he imagined how The Bal Shem Tov* would have told it in a similar style.

"My wife and I were going over the day's events last week. She complained about my sister.

'I called your sister, Rachel, today and right in the middle of our conversation she told me she had an in-coming call and hung up on me. I hate it when she does that. It makes me feel so second class.'

I told my wife that very morning God and I had been talking together. When I noticed in-coming e-mail flashing on my screen, I put God on hold to check it.

I hope God is more forgiving of me than you are of my sister, and I pray that I won't get so distracted next time God and I are talking."

Rabbi Israel ben Eliezer (1698-1760), known as the founder of Hasidic Judaism, was famous for his stories.

Hammer Head

The newly minted clergyperson volunteered at a local Habitat for Humanity build. The master carpenter noticed him struggling with the hammer.

"The hammer handle is about 15 inches long. It is important to hold it down here, away from the head, to use it most effectively," advised the carpenter.

Another volunteer wondered when the new minister would recognize that the distance from his own head to his heart was just a couple of inches longer than a hammer handle and that his effectiveness in ministry would also depend on moving away from his head.

How do I see the interconnectedness of the
entire universe?
How can I enlarge my view of the Gracious
Mystery, the Holy One of many names?

Star Bucks Techies

Jesus and the God of Abraham and Sarah are sitting over coffee at Star Bucks discussing technology. An angel in a gossamer blouse, jeans and flip-flops joins them.

"Hey, I have a question about my GPS."

Jesus interrupts, "I love those new God Positioning Systems. I think they must be a terrific tool for pilgrims."

God asks the angel, "Is there a glitch in your GPS?"

"I wanted to download some maps from my computer.. It said the maps for that territory were no longer compatible."

God sprinkled some more cinnamon on his latte and explained, "Some folks are trying to reactivate an old operating system. They've moved to shut down Windows '65. The angel brushed some cinnamon off the table and asked, "Do you mean there are maps I can't access?"

And God said, "You may need a model that does have a more accurate image of who *I Am*."

"Should I upgrade or just switch to a Mac?"

"When windows are shut, you need to get outside and get a larger vista," God replied. "You know *I am* bigger than any one operating system."

The waitperson offered them more free trade coffee and they toasted a God beyond measure.

Markings

UN leader Dag Hammarskjold* writing in
his journal, <u>Markings</u>, published after his death,
let the world glimpse the inner life of a remarkable
man of action. His now well-known prayer,
> *For all that has been, thanks.*
> *For all that will be, yes,*
had always deeply moved the monastery's teacher.

"It works for a little boy at his birthday party as
well as it does for the old man on his deathbed,"
he explained when admirers asked about his own
equanimity.

* *Nobel laureate Dag Hammarskjöld (1905–1961), was the second Secretary-General of the United Nations (1953 -1961).*

Perspective

The good neighbor took a plate of Christmas cookies to the eccentric couple next door. The husband answered the door.

"My wife's under the table."

With some concern and hesitation, the neighbor inquired, "Is she all right?"

"Oh, she's just checking out how the Christmas tree looks from our dog's point of view."

In order to appreciate another's perspective, we may have to step away from our customary stance in order to be open to respect and dialog.

Life is full of rough and smooth spots.
How am I handling the ups and downs?
To whom do I turn when things get
rough?
With whom do I share my joy?

Antiques Roadshow

The old nun loved to watch Public Broadcasting's
The Antiques Roadshow after her day of volunteer
work at the shelter. She would even leave the Sisters
at evening prayer to watch it, much to the annoyance
of the other nuns. Finally, at the request of the group,
the superior confronted her about her disruptive, and,
she suggested, possibly addictive, behavior.

Sister wasn't upset by the misunderstanding. "Do you
see how excited these folks get when they discover
their attic junk is really a treasure worth thousands of
dollars? Every day at the shelter I walk with people who
think they are junk. This show is my prayer that some
day each of my *junkies* will find their own worth in the
eyes of God, themselves, and me."

The nuns decided their community prayer time
could include some **PBS** programming.

Medical Musings

The master reluctantly went to see the doctor at the insistence of his disciples. He didn't spend much time worrying about his health.

When he returned to the monastery his answers to the questions of his concerned students raised other questions, as usual.

"What eye test can diagnose the prejudices of the heart?"

"What if your spiritual director recommended icing your enlarged ego four times a day with 15 minutes of contemplation?"

"Would insurance cover PT if it were Prayer Time to restore your soul's health?"

"What if the critical care unit became uncritical and only offered praise?"

The disciples thought they might not encourage him to visit the doctor again anytime soon.

What is the sound of... ?

The teacher loved to propose riddles to her young novices. "What 1964 lyrics by Paul Simon name the rarest and finest treasure that is free, but from which most people flee?"

The date made it ancient history to most of the students and they struggled to find an answer. She added a hint, "It is decidedly countercultural today."

One *delayed vocation* student tentatively suggested what he thought, "Sounds of Silence?"

The teacher was pleased and added to iPod-loving students, "It is in the silence that we hear God speak."

The red designer sports car has its springs
on the outside.

How resilient am I?

What helps me bounce back?

Which Car Are You Driving?

Great grandpa drove a Packard because he swore it was the best car in the world. Today Warren, Ohio's only memory of Packard is in a museum and a concert hall bearing the name of its once-famous industry.

Granddad drove a Studebaker in college because it was the coolest design. The Studebaker mansion is now just a restaurant in the car's hometown of South Bend, Indiana.

Mom loved her Oldsmobile convertible. "In My Merry Oldsmobile" is now just a vintage song in the file of golden oldies.

The shape of our dream cars, like our dreams, alters in time with our changing appreciation. If we don't retool our dreams, we may find ourselves stuck in the past.

Song and Dance

What do a Shaker sister and a Sufi dervish have in common? They could both sing and dance the *Shaker Melody* because they know the sacredness of dance.

'Tis the gift to be simple, 'tis the gift to be free,

'Tis the gift to come down where we ought to be,

And when we find ourselves in the place just right,

'Twill be in the valley of love and delight.

When true simplicity is gain'd,

To bow and to bend we shan't be asham'd,

To turn, turn will be our delight,

Till by turning, turning we come out right.

I seem to run around and around in the fashion of a headless chicken. The dance of busy, the dance of more, and the dance of consumerism are not sacred dances.

Coke

The master always smiled when he saw the Coca-Cola delivery truck emblazoned with, "It's the real thing."

He would remind his students of St. Thomas Aquinas who, at the age of 42, mystically experienced God so powerfully that he declared that all his writings were but straw compared to the "real thing." Then the master would challenge them to name what was real for them.

St. Paul said that there were three things that last: faith, hope and love. What are the really real things in our lives? Checking our calendar and checkbook may give us some clues. The evidence may not support our original speculation.

SPLIT PERSONALITY
7/30/06

The butterfly has an unmatched pair of wings.
Do I appreciate the different parts of me?
How do I react when my expectations
don't match reality?

Sudoku

Noting how Japanese Sudoku had become a world-wide craze, the leader at the Shinto shrine asked the group of visiting tourists if they had the Sudoku model of God. They appeared confused by the question that was not part of the planned tour.

"Do you enjoy Sudoku?"

Several heads nodded.

"Do you work long to find the right answer?"

Again heads nodded.

"Many visitors think that way about God. You may enjoy the puzzle of God, but you must know that there is no one answer. In fact, there is no answer book."

Many visitors chose to hold on to their sure truths and take quick photos before boarding the tour bus for the next stop.

Life may feel more safe when we are certain we have the right answers, but when we know we don't know, we are more likely to experience the wonder of the Holy.

Economics 101

In early 2009 the banks, mortgages, the Dow Jones, and the NASDAQ all pointed to a disastrous economic downturn in the U.S. economy. Congress and President Obama's administration rushed to create an economic stimulus package to forestall further decline.

At the same time the German Pope, dismayed over the declining Catholic church membership and influence in Europe and the United States, reintroduced an old package to forestall further decline.

Using a unique ecclesiastical accounting system, indulgences came back in favor as a stimulus package for the faithful.

Declines send some folks to the CPA, others to CPR. The selection must be based on an accurate diagnosis of the problem. Is there a CT scan for faith or the economy?

Howz that spelled?

The speaker at the drug treatment program passed around small, gray rock spheres and asked if anyone knew what they were. One person finally ventured a guess, "Is it a geode?"

The speaker agreed and juggled the rock balls in the air, "Pretty ugly, huh? If we could look inside, we would something very different." She held some polished slices of geodes up to the light to the surprise of the group.

"Well, guess what? You may be feeling like you are ugly, no good at this moment, but what God loves is the inside that God knows is beautiful."

Unslouching, and with a spark in her eye, one person said, "Oh, you said it was spelled G-O-D, didn't you?"

When people admired her geode necklace, the speaker explained that it was one of her favorite symbols of God because of the way one person once spelled geode.

God invites us to see beyond the rough exterior to each person's interior beauty that mirrors God's.

What boundaries do I have?

Should I create some appropriate ones or
take down some others?

What old boundaries have opened for me
to pass through?

African Clinic

After a brief visit to a nearby mosque, the stately African man returned to his place in line at the visiting Christian missionary medical clinic.

An eager young member of the clinic's evangelical team approached him. The young man enthusiastically "preached" to the old man in broken French and gave him a copy of a pocket-sized New Testament in French.

Triumphantly, the eager preacher turned to the white-haired volunteer receptionist and said, "I have just told him all about God."

She turned to the patient and apologized for the young man's apparent disrespect and, in perfect French, spoke softly, "I, too, am a person of prayer. Tell me about your prayer."

We often preach better by listening than by proclaiming our personal version of the truth.

Training Methods

The veterinary professor was critiquing a well-known television dog trainer. She said domination was his approach to dog training. "He would never be able to teach a dog tricks because to do that you must bond with your dog and develop trust so that the dog knows what you want and wants to do it out of love, not fear."

Does that seem like good marriage advice, child psychology, peace-making, theology, or is it simply a veterinary observation?

How May I Help You?

Rajiv was filled with relief when he passed the English exam and could begin working for the American company's customer service department.

He would be able to ride his bicycle through the traffic-filled streets of Hyderabad and earn more money than he had ever imagined possible.

On his first day, he was astounded at the noise level in the warehouse room of cubicles for the customer service staff. His anxious heart pounded, adding its roar in his ears.

Then he remembered his grandmother often repeating the Lord Vishnu's advice to Prince Arjuna, "Enter into the din of battle with your heart at the lotus feet of the Lord." For the first time, he understood the value of that advice from The Bagavadgita, and began his new job from his own deep, quiet center.

The stories from all sacred scriptures can show us how to live peacefully and compassionately, if we take them off the pages and into our hearts.

In oriental painting the concept of "sunyata,"
emptiness, is a key element in design.
How can I create more empty space in
my crowded life ?
How can I can be more open and aware?

The Book of Common Prayer

A socialite member of his parish came to see the rector, well-known in the area as a man of prayer. She looked stunning as ever; the gilt-edged pages of her Book of Common Prayer coordinated with her accessories.

She sat ruffling the pages a bit awkwardly as she asked for help in learning to pray. The rector listened with close attention for some time. His question startled her, "You look lovely today. Have you ever shopped at our St. John's Next-to-New Shop?"

Her cheeks flushed as she declared, "Father, I would never think of buying second-hand clothes."

"Of course not, my dear. So how is that you are content with second-hand prayers? Put the book away and talk and listen to God in your heart."

Smell the Flowers

The nurse admired the bouquet of spring flowers beautifully arranged in Uncle George's hospital room.

"They lift my spirits; they smell so fresh and are simply marvelous."

His daughter revealed that they were silk.

Seeing is not always about believing; the senses can reinforce the reality we expect.

Plane Talk

The Christian teller of sacred stories was seated next to a Hasidic rabbi on a long flight from California. They began exploring their own favorites among the vast array of Hasidic tales. There was much joy in finding a shared interest in story.

As the plane began its descent, the rabbi expressed his appreciation to the teller. In summary he said, "You are a nice lady, and I am a nice man, but I am better than you." Thinking it was probably a gender issue, the teller invited further explanation: "It's because God chose us."

The root of all evil is not always money as is sometimes claimed. It is in believing that we alone are God's specially chosen ones. By limiting God's choice to our particular tribe, nation, religion or political belief, we make a small God and, far too often, big arguments and big wars.

The decaying shingles create their own pattern.
What patterns do I see in myself?
Where is some of my exterior decaying?
Am I willing to expose what's below
my surface?

Salt of the Hearth

When Jesus was being well-received in his public ministry, Mary wasn't hesitant to take credit for some of his stories. One morning when the women gathered around the well, she had them all smiling knowingly.

"Did you hear the one he told about 'you are the salt of the hearth, the light of the world'? We all know where *that* came from, don't we?"

The women put down their water jugs. All their lives they had collected dung to burn in their cooking fires, and each kept salt by the hearth to increase the heat and light of the burning dung. They knew where the story came from and what it meant.

"I guess some of those city folks don't use salt and dung the way we do. They thought he said, 'salt of the earth,' not the hearth as he meant," Mary said. And the women all laughed out loud together.

The word in Aramaic for earth and hearth is the same. Jesus watched Mary use salt to make the dung burn brighter and hotter.
Knowing he meant the salt of the hearth, *we can hear the call to be chemical agents for change, to transform the negative and bring light into the darkness.*

Namaste

The woman slowed her car and pulled off the side of the highway to take a photo. A police officer drove up behind her.

Nervously, she had to explain her purpose. "I want a picture of that *Pass It On* billboard because it fits perfectly into the theme of our retreat center."

The officer looked at the image of the American artist, Norman Rockwell, painting one of his famous *Saturday Evening Post* covers. He smiled as he read the message: "He saw the best in us."

"That's sometimes hard to do in my job," he observed.

"Well, at our retreat center it is a theme. We have a mirror on the wall with a frame that says, "Mirror the good you see in others, so they will believe it."

"Makes me think of something we say at the end of our yoga class, 'Namaste.' I never thought about using it in my police work."

"I use that greeting too to welcome people to our center. I usually have to explain that it means the light and goodness in me honors the light and goodness in you."

The two smiled and bowed to each other appreciatively, and went on their way, honoring goodness and light.

Throw-away art project scraps challenge me to look at what I think is only junk.

When I am discouraged, what do I do?

How should I rethink some old values?

What story or photo, drawing or poetry of your own would you add here for your pondering?

 *Illusions are fun to doodle, but hard to recognize in ourselves.*

*What questions do you want to ask yourself?
What questions would you like to ask your
spouse, friend, parent, child?*

sOs '07

Stories can lift your spirits and
inspire you to look more closely
and see farther.

How can I lighten up?
Where do my dreams take me?

Photos and Art

Photography using my Fuji S5000 digital camera helps me discover beauty all around as I look at the familiar with fresh eyes. I have studied Miksang Photography and it influences how I see. My pen and ink drawing and painting with oil pastel always surprise me. As I gaze, I see more; I am soul snorkeling. As I pay attention to that process, I discover the voice of the Holy One within and everywhere.

Cover: Crooked Lake, Conroy, Michigan
Opposite title page: Temecula, California,
Opposite *Contents*: Toledo, Ohio,
P. 2: Art glass, Ouray, Colorado
P. 6: Toledo Botanical Garden
P. 10: Siesta Beach Key, Sarasota, Florida
P. 14: University of British Columbia, Vancouver, BC
P. 18: Breckenridge, Colorado
P. 22: Oil pastel, 2006, celebrating a grandchild's
    birth, "The heavens are alive with the sound
    of music"
P. 26: Railroad station steps, Egham, Surrey, UK
P. 30: Second Street, Long Beach, California
P. 34: Oil pastel, 2004, "Split Personality,"
P. 38: Asilomar State Park, Pacific Grove, California
P. 42: Toledo Botanical Garden
P. 46: Millersville, Maryland
P. 49: Anderson Ranch, Snowmass, Colorado
P. 52: Pen and ink, 2007, "Flight of Fancy"

Warning Label:

These stories are the work of a storyteller/storylistener
and come with no guarantee. They may be injurious to
your mind, body, soul health if taken too lightly or taken
too seriously.

Recommended dosage:

One or two stories as needed taken under a child's
supervision. Take photos one at a time with wine or juice.

In case of overdose:

Rent a brainless video, go for a swim, or immerse yourself in
some volume of Nieitzsche, Dostoevsky, Beckett or Dr. Seuss.

In case of emergency:

E-mail the teller: soulsnorkeling@gmail.com

Ingredients:

These stories are inspired by the style of Indian Jesuit
storyteller, psychotherapist, and author, Anthony de Mello.
He might smile, but is not responsible for their effect.

Made in the USA